Pudsey
in old picture postcards volume 2

Ruth Strong

European Library ZALTBOMMEL / THE NETHERLANDS

GB ISBN 90 288 4903 3

© 1990 European Library – Zaltbommel/The Netherlands

Second edition, 2001: this second edition is purely a reprint; date references
are taken from the original date of publication.

European Library
post office box 49
NL – 5300 AA Zaltbommel/The Netherlands
telephone: 0031 418 513144
fax: 0031 418 515515
e-mail:publisher@eurobib.nl

INTRODUCTION

My first reaction to the prospect of doing a second volume of 'Pudsey in old picture postcards' was 'however can I find another seventy-six photographs?' Yet once feelers began to be put out lots of new photographs were offered by many generous people. These contributions account for about a third of the contents. The rest come from the collections of Fulneck Museum and the Pudsey Civic Society between whom the royalties from the sale of this volume will be divided.

The photographs were nearly all taken between 1880 and 1930, far enough removed from the present to reveal many changes but not so distant from the Pudsey our grandparents described as to be entirely remote. Many photographs will generate nostalgic reminiscences, especially as so much of the old town has gone. In writing the captions I have struggled to think of different words for 'demolished' which I felt was becoming grossly overused. This tells its own story. So much of old Pudsey, as of other towns, has been destroyed through lack of historical awareness and an over-zealous commitment to slum clearance.

This collection of photographs has been arranged roughly by subject, beginning with street scenes and the park followed by chapel and sporting activities, housing, transport, shops, the village of Fulneck, schools, civic events and celebrations, and last but not least, industry. Although the collection cannot hope to be comprehensive, nor even balanced, yet something of the optimism and confident sense of progress which pervaded the town throughout this period comes through strongly.

Pudsey had been a separate township at least since the Domesday Survey of 1086-1087. Yet until the latter half of the nineteenth century it had little effective local government. Then between 1880 and 1930 civic amenities developed fast. In 1885 Pudsey became the centre of a parliamentary constituency, in 1899 it received a Charter of Incorporation enabling it to have its own mayor and corporation, in 1909 it was granted its own Commission of the Peace (ie. its own Court) and in the following twenty years acquired public baths and a childrens' playground. Moreover, the economy of the town experienced a major transformation during the fifty years. In 1880 Pudsey was suffering the final death throes of the traditional woollen industry. This industry had been based on small independent clothiers who wove their pieces on handlooms, usually in their own homes, and sold them to the merchants at Leeds Coloured Cloth Hall. But by 1880 the powerloom had almost ousted the time-honoured handloom and in 1889 the Coloured Cloth Hall closed. Then woollen mills, instead of being owned by companies of up to fifty small clothiers became family concerns. Moreover the manufacture of worsteds became almost as important as that of woollens and these firms were traditionally individual initiatives, or small partnerships. And by 1880 boot and shoe manufacturing and also tanning were important local industries. Nearly all these new, large-scale employers lived locally and gave generously to local 'causes', especially to the building of chapels and Sunday Schools.

Much of the wealth created within the town was therefore reinvested in local amenities. This liaison between economic prosperity and civic pride perhaps reached its zenith in the early twentieth century. By 1930 the local boot and shoe industry was in steep decline and the woollen and worsted industries were battling against recurrent economic slumps. The vision of eternal progress was faltering. Pudsey's last major manifestation of civic progress was in 1937 when it annexed the Urban Districts of Calverley and Farsley. Then in 1974 came a keen humiliation with the town's incorporation into the massive Leeds Metropolitan District.

Pudsey's identity was also being undermined by improvements in transport. More people worked in Leeds and Bradford and there was a tendency for local employers to get away from Pudsey's dust and grime, the source of their wealth, as soon as possible to havens such as Harrogate and Morecombe. With a few notable exceptions wealthy, public-spirited men in the mould of W.D. Scales, James Stillings and Thomas and Alfred Lund became less common as the century progressed.

It would, however, be wrong to end on a note of gloom.

Today Pudsey is experiencing something of a revival. The vacuum left by the declining textile industry has been largely filled by light industry dulling the impact of unemployment crises. Clean air legislation too has had a profound effect on the quality of life in the town. Proximity to unspoilt countryside, as well as to Leeds and Bradford, its inherent community spirit and its wealth of solid stone houses has made Pudsey a popular place to live. It has one of the most resilient housing markets in West Yorkshire. The man who in 1834 wrote of Pudsey as *inhabited almost entirely by clothiers and notwithstanding its elevated situation... is one of the dirtiest and most unpleasant* (towns) *in the district* would be hard pressed to recognise the same town today.

I would like to thank the following without whose help this book could not have been written:
Fulneck Museum, Pudsey Civic Society, Margaret Barrett, Roland Hepworth, Pat Holmes, Joan Mort, Alfred Parkin, Emily Read, Jean Saville, Terry Wetherald and Rita Wilson who have lent photographs, and also John Brayshaw, George Butterfield, Margaret and Jack Calvert, Vera Cruse, Hilda Hannan, Daphne and Philip Keighley and Wilfred Pollard who have helped in other ways.

1. Waver Green, in the centre of Pudsey, was once part of the town's common land. When this photograph was taken in the 1880s it had become Pudsey's first market place. The huts in the foreground were occupied by Job Wilcocks hot pea saloon (Job Cocks pey 'oil), 'Tripey Ross' and the grocer James Galloway. There was also Jonathan Brayshaws photographic studio, Billy Dibbs boot repairing hut and the town's first fish and chip shop. In 1883 James Galloway bought the corner shop of Commercial Buildings, on the right of the picture. The shop had previously belonged to the druggist, Joseph Walker, and it was many years before the old name 'Druggists Corner' gave way to 'Galloways Corner'. Today it is just 'The Lights'. Waver Green was finally cleared of its delapidated huts in 1889 and two years later the Midland Bank was built on the corner site. The building on the left was Pudsey's first fire station with the offices of Pudsey's Local Board of Health, the fore-runner of the Town Council, above.

2. This interesting shop must have been demolished before 1903 when Pudsey's new Post Office was built on the site. The Post Office moved to the present building in 1957. Beyond Waver House was a road which widened out into the market place, which by 1890 had replaced that shown in plate 1. Look at the goods for sale at Waver House, mattings, oil cloths, window blinds, family mourning, dress and mantle trimmings. It doesn't take much imagination to picture the domestic lives of the customers. And look closely at the little group outside the house door. Although the picture is blurred there looks to be a coffin and men with bowed heads. In old style funerals when the undertaker had screwed down the lid the coffin was carried outside and placed on chairs. Then the mourners gathered round to sing Luther's hymn before the procession formed to wend its way to the funeral proper.

3. These are the shops seen in the distance in plate 2, although the photograph must have been taken rather later as trams didn't come to Pudsey until 1908. At this time the first shop was Jacksons house furnishers, next was Sam Wilsons music shop, then came Battye's the plumbers, Joe Hanson the hairdresser and Willie Davy, confectioner and pork butcher. Later Willie Davy concentrated on the bakery side of the business, hawking his bread and cakes round the town in baskets. Later one of the shops was occupied by Beermans, Pudsey's first fully qualified electricians. The shops were eventually pulled down to open up the market place to Church Lane and, at the far end, provide a site for the Woolworth block of shops. Further up Church Lane is the Unitarian Church. The tower was later taken down when it became unsafe. The two houses behind have also been pulled down. In the distance is the tower of Pudsey Church.

4. Here is Pudsey's second market place, now incorporated into the town centre car park. On market days, and especially on Saturday nights, the stalls were a very different sight from the drear scene above. All came alive with colour and bustle, with Oliver Hudsons sweet stall, Sharps lino and carpet strip stall, Hammonds toyshop, Ross's tripe shop, a coloured man selling patent cough mixture, Schofields greengrocery and countless other stalls all noisily touting for trade. On Saturday nights the atmosphere was enhanced by the Salvation Army Band. In the background is the back of Stonsfield Square where many firemen lived, close to the fire station. In the 1930s the market place was enlarged and thereafter the market consisted entirely of temporary stalls. The old huts were demolished and the tenants offered alternative accommodation in the newly built row of shops in Robin Lane, almost opposite the Manor Hall.

MARKET PLACE. PUDSEY

5. This photograph of the market place in 1952, the only picture in the book taken after 1930, has been included as so much has altered in the last thirty-eight years. First, the car park is almost empty! On market days there were no cars at all as it was filled with stalls. You can see some of the stalls in the background. And the Picture House is now Gateways superstore. Two shops were incorporated into the front of the old Picture House, Crossleys fashions on the right and Rogers sweets and tobacconist on the left. Programmes changed twice weekly and on Saturday afternoon there was a children's matinee with a thrilling cowboy serial. The episode always ended at some cliff hanging moment of suspence. The parade of shops on the left was newly built in 1952. Today only Woolworths remains. The others were Wilsons (china, kitchenware etc.), Speights (greengrocers, only recently changed hands), Purdys (fabrics) and Elsters (shoes).

6. Here is Church Lane from Druggist's Corner, looking west, decorated for the Carnival. In the foreground are Commercial Buildings, with Galloways the grocers on the corner and Bennetts, another grocer, at Lion House at the other end. The elegant standard on the left held the electric cable for the trams. At first the trams had to negotiate a sharp right-hand turn at the bottom of Lidget Hill. Frequently trams rattling down the hill came off the lines. In 1920 therefore the line was relaid so the corner could be taken diagonally. The relaid line is just visible. Beyond Lion House Dr. Byrd's garden reached down to the road, where Boots is today. Then, after the new parade of shops, comes Church Lane Picture House. It opened in December 1920. This was Pudsey's second picture house, the first, Mr. Green's Palace in Lowtown, had already been open ten years.

7. This is a close-up of James Galloway's shop, taken about eighty years ago, with James Galloway proudly standing in the doorway. The business had been started by his father, another James, in a market hut on Waver Green. It is just possible to read the notice above the shop: 'Provision Merchant, Grocer and Corn Merchant.' Many people kept pigs and poultry so the supply of animal feed was an important part of the business. Purchases were delivered with the help of Punch and Paddy, two horses kept in a field in Boggard Lane (now Mount Pleasant). Periodically they managed to knock down the wall and trot up to the shop, frequently in the middle of the night. James Galloway was quite used to being knocked up by the police in the early hours! The little boy looking rather quizzically at the camera, Frank Galloway, died of scarlet fever in Calverley Joint Fever Hospital shortly after the photograph was taken. Notice the early telephone number over the door.

Lowtown, Pudsey

5310

8. At a casual glance Lowtown has changed little since this photograph was taken about seventy years ago. But look more closely and you see there is no Clifton Hill. Instead, just above the Pudsey and Stanningley News offices and printing works is Albert Farnells hairdressers shop. Then comes Alberts Garage, newly built on the site of Thompson Cravens cobblers hut. Motor cars and wagons were beginning to take over from horse-drawn traffic. The garage is now transformed into Cravens Fish Restaurant. Above the garage is Gallons, a multiple grocer, then comes Winterburns, ironmongers and tinplate works. Next is a butchers, at one time Oliver Appleyards, later Firths (who introduced cheap, frozen meat into the town) and now Dalbys. Then comes the entry to Hammerton Fold, now renamed Booths Yard after James Booths grocers shop on the corner. Notice the cobbled 'crossing' in the foreground, very necessary when roads were 'unmade' and most traffic still horse-drawn.

Chapeltown, Pudsey

9. This picture shows Chapeltown before the cenotaph was erected in 1922. On the far side of the wall and railings in the left foreground was a derelict graveyard. It had belonged to Pudsey's All Saint's Chapel of Ease. It was estimated that between 1755 (when the graveyard was already fifty years old) and 1814 there had been no fewer than 3,980 interments in the tiny plot of under a quarter of an acre. All Saint's Chapel was eventually demolished in 1879 but there was so much local sentiment about the graveyard that it was left to rot for another fifty years. People called it 'Pot Heaven' because of all the broken pots and debris dumped there. The spire in the distance belongs to the Congregational Church (plate 30). The new parade of shops in the foreground catered for most needs. There was Ernest Jones, grocer and hardware dealer, Golightlys the chemist (this is still a chemist today), J.W. Birks, hatter and outfitter and Squire Johnson, joiner, builder, house furnisher and undertaker.

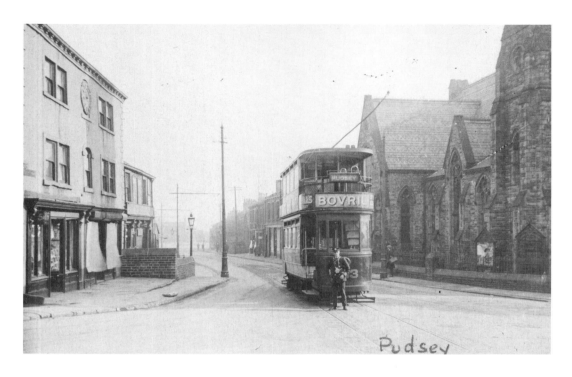

Pudsey

10. This photograph is taken from the junction of Greenside, Chapeltown and Chapeltown Top, the terminus of the Leeds tram. On the right is the north side of the Congregational Church seen in plate 30. Just visible in the distance, facing up Chapeltown, is the detached stone house where 'Havercake Wilson' lived. Its address was originally '1 Parsonage Fold', the house being the solitary surviving dwelling in a cluster of old property adjoining the old parsonage (plate 33). William Wilson made his havercakes, on a huge, red-hot stone slab, a yard square. He hawked them round the town shouting 'Oatcakes, Oatcakes', and they were also very popular in local pubs before the arrival of potato crisps. An old map of Pudsey in the 1740s shows a double pair of stocks, standing under a broad tree, just to the right of this photograph, on the edge of Stocks Green. This Green was later reflected in the names Greenside, Greentop and Greenbottom (an early name for Smalewell Road).

11. Here is another picture of Chapeltown before the cenotaph was built. It was taken from the Chapeltown end of Carlisle Road. The little hut in the right foreground is still there. Beyond is part of Greenside School and then, apparently in the school playground, are two buildings. The larger one, a big, three-storeyed house, was a grocers and off-licence, formerly occupied by a Mrs. Rankin but latterly by Thomas Henry Illingworth. Mrs. Rankin did a particularly good trade in beer, in 1904 getting through five twenty-eight gallon barrels a week. These houses were demolished when the cenotaph was built and the site incorporated into Greenside School yard. The house in the left foreground is the end of School Street, but the houses behind were pulled down when Sparrow Park was made. Notice the horse's nosebag hanging from the cart shaft. This was attached to the horse's head so he could champ contentedly away at his dinner.

12. The next two pictures are of Fartown. This one is taken shortly after Pudsey Church's Fartown Sunday School was built on the corner of Carlisle Road in 1923. Behind the sign for Bentley's Yorkshire Brewery lies the Fleece Inn yard and beyond, hidden behind the building in the foreground, the pair of three-storeyed (garret) houses and adjoining shop which survive today. Herbert Salter, who had this shop for many years after the Second World War, began his business in the shop, plastered with posters, across the road. The next row of houses belonged to James Banks & Sons, woollen and worsted manufacturers of Fartown (previously Claughton Garth) Mill. They backed onto the mill yard. A similar row opposite, Banks Buildings, remains today. Behind the gas lamp are the gates of the mill yard with a mill house adjoining. Then comes a row of four eighteenth-century cottages with a larger cottage squashed in the corner. Only the two outer cottages are visible. A single earth privy was shared by all five families (thirty-four people) as late as the 1920s.

13. This view is slightly further up Fartown with the mill house and old cottages in the right foreground. It is also a rather later date as electric street lamps have replaced the gas lamps. Alfred Parkin who grew up in the end cottage, hidden behind the mill house, remembers how his mother could make a good dinner for seven from a quarter of a pound of corned beef, with onions and potatoes. She made dinner for 'Old Elizabeth' who lived opposite for 3d a week, took in washing, and mashed tea for the workers at Fartown Mill charging ½d for a pint pot. For 3d a week they could sit round her kitchen table. She also baked two stone of flour every Wednesday, making bread for the week, and flat cakes, which were tilted up outside the door to cool. Fartown Sunday School (now Fartown Christian Fellowship) is hidden behind J.W. Jackson's outfitters on the corner of Carlisle Road. After the failure of Joseph Banks & Sons in 1929 the Fartown Mill property was sold to the tanner, Edgar Handley and later to Asda Stores Ltd. Then the eighteenth century cottages and the mill houses were pulled down making way for Asda's car park.

22102 OVERLAND
AIR VIEWS

CHAPELTOWN. PUDSEY

HOLLIDAY
NEWSAGENT

14. This aerial photograph of Chapeltown was taken in the 1920s, shortly after the cenotaph was built on the site of the old All Saint's graveyard (plate 9). In the right foreground are New Street Mills (plate 75), and Greenside station. Grove House can just be seen in the trees, although the parade of shops at the bottom of the garden had yet to be built. Red Court, the home of Pudsey's first woman mayor, Mrs. Elizabeth Lund, was then newly built in the grounds. At the extreme left the Congregational Church and graveyard are just visible, and to their right is the Golden Lion bowling green, now a car park. At the top left-hand corner is St. Lawrence Cricket Club's Tofts Road ground and beyond some of the chapel cricket fields. These were later combined to make Queens Park. Every chapel had two, sometimes three cricket teams and competition in the Sunday School League was keen. Pudsey Church stands out boldly. Originally with accommodation for two thousand it was, and is, the largest church or chapel in Pudsey.

15. Here is another view of Pudsey Church, seen from the park promenade and taken in 1903. The promenade was planned as the main feature of Pudsey's new park when it was opened in 1889. It was 240 feet long and 45 feet wide, overlooking the rest of the park, the bandstand, the lake, the huge fountain and the intricate network of paths enclosing the lawns, shrubberies and flowerbeds. All self-respecting towns had a promenade where on Sunday afternoons people could be seen in their Sunday best in a pleasant arcadian setting. It was also where the boys sized up the girls — and vica versa. After the First World War two guns and a large shell, a gift from the War Office, were placed on the promenade. But it was an unpopular move and they soon disappeared. During the Second World War a huge marquee was erected in Pudsey feast week and entertainment provided to encourage support for the 'Holidays at Home' campaign. But that was something of an Indian summer. Promenading was no longer popular and Pudsey's promenade is now reduced to a broad path.

THE PARK, PUDSEY.

16. This photograph is also taken from the park promenade, looking in the other direction. The bandstand, given by Pudsey's Liberal MP, Briggs Priestley, and the greenhouses were designed by Charles Sebastian Nelson of Fulneck. He was also architect for the park lodge. The greenhouses were rebuilt, 'as far as the woodwork' was concerned in 1908, this time by Jowett Kendall & Son, a local firm which was to win many civic contracts. Recently they have been replaced by a large modern conservatory. Originally it was planned to build public baths to the left of the greenhouses. Pudsey's Local Board of Health declared that 'in past years many lives have been lost through bathers indiscreetly entering deep water in our dams and reservoirs' and recommended 'a good bath at small cost'. With this in mind Pudsey's Sanitary Committee visited Sowerby's 'splendid baths'. But the prospect of a yet higher rate proved too daunting and Pudsey had to wait another thirty-nine years for its public baths.

17. There was no problem knowing what to do with small children in the afternoon. George and Mary (named after the King and Queen), residents on the park lake, were always ready for tit-bits. The lake was serpentine shaped with an island of stones in the middle and a hut at the edge for nesting. It was also well stocked with sticklebacks which were kept busy keeping out of the way of fishing nets made from old net curtains. The lake was only a foot deep at the edge, and three feet deep in the middle, so it normally didn't matter much when children fell in. But very occasionally a child was drowned. So in 1935 the lake was replaced by the Jubilee Gardens, a delightful maze of rockeries and streams, paths and bridges. Sadly this proved too costly to maintain and the site is now a rose garden. In the background, on the left, is Radcliffe, probably built by James Stillings, Pudsey's first mayor. You can just see the conservatory where every Christmas his wife entertained the old ladies from the Salvation Army.

18. People were encouraged to make gifts to the new park. W.D. Scales, boot and shoe manufacturer of Grove House, as Pudsey's main employer, gave this fountain. It was a substantial creation, standing to the north of the lake, costing £170 and being eighteen feet high and eleven feet broad at the base. You can just read the inscription: 'This fountain was erected and dedicated to the public by W.D. Scales 1899.' Mr. Scales was a great temperance advocate so a water fountain would be a very appropriate gift. On each side was a lion's head from which ran the water, and a bell-shaped bronze cup secured by a chain. Originally the fountain was surrounded by paths and flower beds, as in the picture. Later, however, it was almost hidden amongst mature trees and shrubs. It became neglected and was demolished some years ago.

BOWLING GREEN, PUDSEY PARK

19. Pudsey park had been open nineteen years before the bowling green was made. Until then the only bowling greens were attached to public houses. The initiative for a public green came from the Mechanics Institute which wanted it in the park. But the Council, not wanting to detract from the park amenities, wanted it on the Recreation Ground, an expanse of waste ground, the site of the present children's playground and sports centre car park. A meeting was planned of eight Council members and three from the 'Mechanics'. The Council thought they had it 'in the bag'. But only one councillor turned up so the 'Mechanics' plan prevailed and the park site was chosen. The green and pavilion, opened in July 1908, cost £400. They were the gift of the ex-mayor, Alderman William Croft Forrest, woollen manufacturer and spinner of Prospect Mills. The pavilion was designed by Jowett Kendall & Son.

20. A sunny afternoon in June 1907 at Pudsey St. Lawrence. The match was probably 'The Match of the Season' between the Saints and Stanningley and Farsley Britannia. There was a big gate and it was said the cheering could be heard in Stanningley. The older ladies sit under the high boundary wall, sheltered from the prevailing wind, as they still do today. The club moved to the new ground on Tofts Road in 1889 when its old ground opposite the Park Hotel was bought by Pudsey Local Board of Health for a park. The Saints had just built a £150 pavilion in the new fashionable, and practical, glazed brick with an open balcony on the roof for the benefit of VIPs. This description also fits the pavilion in the picture suggesting that it was rebuilt in the new ground. The pavilion was sited diagonally across the corner of the field, directly in front of the present entrance. Across the pitch there was originally a second pavilion for the private use of an important benefactor of the club, W.D. Scales.

21. The Fulneck Single Sisters Tennis Club. The Club was formed just before the First World War by the Single Sisters Labouress, Miss Clemens. She is sitting third from the left in the middle row. She felt that as the Fulneck Institute catered only for young men there was nothing for young girls to do. So the girls paid 3d a week for a piece of waste ground, near where the Headmaster's house now stands. The ground was levelled and made into a cinder tennis court. Predictably the girls usually returned home ready for a good wash. Mrs. Willey, the minister's wife, the elegant lady in the centre, was the non-playing president. On her left is Mrs. Lumby, the superintendant of the Girls Sunday School. It was a very gentle game which Miss Clemens taught her girls. To serve, the ball was deliberately placed in the middle of the racket and gently propelled forward. Single Sisters who went to Pudsey's Secondary School had to learn a much more aggressive game.

22. This photograph, taken in about 1924, shows Ebenezer Primitive Methodist football team. That year they were the proud winners of the Pudsey Football Sunday School League's special cup for 'Gentlemanly Conduct'. The cup had been given by Sim. Myers, a well-loved councillor and mayor, remembered as 'a boy in spirit to the end of his days'. In those days 'young men', todays teenagers, were kept out of mischief by all the activities associated with Sunday Schools and Institutes. There were prized cups to be won in the Sunday School Leagues for football, cricket and billiards. Ebenezer's football pitch was in 'Ike Gont's field', behind the chapel, close to the Pudsey and Stanningley Rugby Club field. The cricket pitch was on the other side of Richardshaw Lane. This photograph was probably taken outside the Ebenezer Institute, under the back of the chapel. Sitting in the middle is the president, Richard Ingham, who in 1923 revived Pudsey's carnival. On his right, with a beard, is Moses Waterhouse, Ebenezer's 'grand old man'.

23. Pudsey Church had one of the earliest scout groups in the country. Baden-Powell founded the Scout movement in 1908 and the following year Pudsey Church's Fartown Sunday School Boy Scouts Union was formed. By 1911 this had developed into the Pudsey Church Scout Patrol. At first the Patrol met three times a week, for Bible study, drill, badge work and, on Saturdays, marches accompanied by two bugles and a drum to places as far afield as Bramhope. By 1913 the Patrol had a drum and fife band. This photograph, taken outside Pudsey Church, shows the vicar, the Rev. Owen French, in the middle. The man on his left is likely to have been Fred Strickland, the first scoutmaster. Next to him is the Church Army officer who, along with the vicar and curate, was instrumental in forming the Patrol. A drum and two bugles can be seen on the front row suggesting that the photograph was taken about 1913. Only after the First World War was this Patrol, and similar groups nationwide, absorbed into the newly formed Boy Scouts Association.

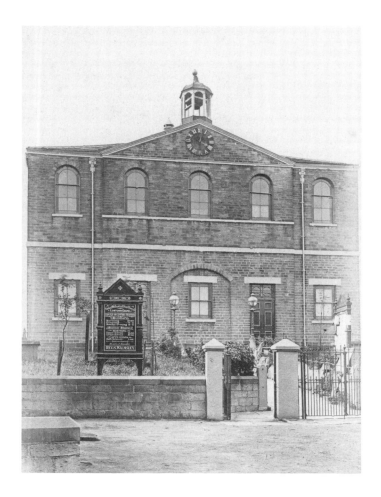

24. Pudsey's 'Clock Chapel', seen here, was Pudsey's second Methodist chapel. It was latterly affectionately known as 'Old Hannahs' after the caretaker. The Methodist's first meeting house, built in 1773, stood on the corner of Manor House Street and Robin Lane. As the Methodist Society grew, to 246 members in 1794, a larger building was needed. So in 1816 this chapel was built on the site of an old barn which in the late seventeenth century had been one of the first meeting places for religious dissenters in Pudsey. In the early days there were three Sunday services, at 10am, 2pm and 5.30pm. Twice a quarter there was an afternoon Love Feast. Early morning Love Feasts were also remembered when the worshippers gathered at the bottom of Lowtown at 6am and sang their way up to Old Hannahs for the Love Feast at 6.30am. By the 1890s the chapel's simple, unassuming architecture was considered old-fashioned, unsuitable for Pudsey's leading Methodist chapel. So in 1897 it closed and within two years the imposing Trinity Church, built on the same foundations, was opened.

25. Here is the fine interior of Trinity Church in 1904, just five years after the church was opened. The church cost £7,700 making it Pudsey's most costly nonconformist place of worship. Thomas Lund of Crawshaw Mills was a major benefactor giving both £1,000 towards the church and also paying for the magnificent organ. He was brother to Alfred Lund, who gave generously to Pudsey Church (plate 40). The interior is dominated by the massive organ and choir, a worthy setting for oratorios and the annual rendering of The Messiah. Sadly the church was closed in 1982 when the congregation was united with St. Andrew's Methodist Church. But it is a tribute to local initiatives and sensitive planning that so much of the original building is retained in its new role as shopping mall and Arts Centre. The exterior is virtually unaltered, as is the stained glass in the windows and the handsome ogee-shaped cast-iron balustrade with its mahogany hand rail, now incorporated into the Arts Centre.

Trinity U.M.F.C. Opening of New Sunday School - March 1911.   Fairbank, Photo

26. The occasion here is obviously the laying of the foundation stones of Trinity's new Upper Sunday School rather than the opening as stated in the caption! The building was called the Manor Hall because it stood on the site of Pudsey's old manor house (plate 32). It cost nearly £6,000, only slightly less than Trinity Church itself, making it the largest Sunday School in the town. The architect was W.H. Dinsley of Manchester who had also designed Trinity Church and the Robin Lane Primitive Methodist Chapel, now St. Andrew's. Pudsey's mayor and mayoress, the president of the Methodist Conference, the architect and contractors, the chapel trustees, choir, teachers and Sunday School scholars processed from Trinity Church to the building site led by Pudsey's Brass Band. The names of these laying the thirty-one foundation stones were commemorated on a brass plate in the school rather than on the stones themselves. The shops in the background are on the site of Pudsey's first Methodist Chapel.

27. The next three photographs are all of Ebenezer Primitive Methodists. The first meetings were held in about 1830, in a cottage on Primrose Hill, a poor district near the bottom of Richardshaw Lane. About the same time a Sunday School was started in the upper room of this house in Cavendish Place. It was probably an old weaving chamber, 'open overall', and also open to the rafters, with plenty of natural ventilation. There was direct access from outside so the weavers, and Sunday School scholars, could reach the garret without tramping through the house. Scholars were not only taught to read, so they could read the Bible, but also to write. For most scholars it was the only education they ever received. One ex-scholar, the Leeds councillor Peter Laycock, remembered how when he left he was given a Bible for always coming to school clean! In 1835 a chapel was built on the east of Richardshaw Lane, about where Richardshaw Lane now crosses the Stanningley by-pass. But the Sunday School continued in this garret for another twenty years.

28. The scholars of Ebenezer Primitive Methodist Sunday School are assembled for their Whit Walk. The photograph is taken outside Ebenezer's second chapel, built in 1865, just below the 1836 chapel. On the right is the 1856 Sunday School. Whit Monday was the climax of weeks of preparation, for singing the new Whitsuntide hymns and for ensuring that the children all had new outfits for the occasion. The scholars met at 1.30pm, each bringing a mug. After the walk the children returned to the schoolroom for tea and clothes baskets full of long buns made by the mothers. The day finished with sports and games in the cricket field. On the right of the picture an older girl has a violin, presumably to accompany the singing. She was probably a member of Luther Gaunt's violin class at Primrose Hill School (plate 64). Ebenezer had previously had its own brass band to accompany the walk but by 1899 it had become detached from the chapel and renamed the Richardshaw Lane Brass Band.

29. Ebenezer's single storeyed Sunday School of 1856 (plate 28), eventually proved too small for the multitude of Sunday School activities and for its four hundred scholars and teachers. So in 1908 a new school was built, and at the same time the chapel enlarged. It was an ambitious project, especially as the chapel served some of the poorest property in Pudsey. Many adults had not the 1s. 1d. for a quarterly class ticket, or money for the Sunday collection, so didn't go to chapel themselves. Yet nearly all the children went to Sunday School. The new school cost over £2,000. It included a large central hall with fifteen classrooms so that for the first time classroom teaching, as in weekday school, was possible. This photograph shows Pudsey's mayoress, Mrs. Joseph Huggan, laying the foundation stone. She is in white in the middle of the crowd. You can just see the chapel on the left. The Sunday School, chapel and the houses in the background were all demolished when the Stanningley ring road was made.

30. Pudsey's United Reformed Church from the south. This fine building was demolished in 1978 since when part of the Sunday School has been made into the chapel. Anchor flats now stand on the site and the Abbeyfield Homes on the old burial ground. Pudsey's United Reformed congregation originated in 1662 when Presbyterians were excluded from the Church of England. Over the centuries the congregation became 'Independent', then 'Congregationalist' and continues today as part of the United Reformed Church. Pudsey's early Presbyterians met in private houses and large barns. In 1708 a meeting house was built behind the present Commercial Hotel. By the end of the century, however, this proved too small so part of Tristram Moss Great Croft, opposite the old meeting house, was bought (for 1s 3d a square yard!) for a chapel and burial ground. The chapel, opened in 1794, was replaced by the handsome gothic building seen above in 1866.

31. The tradition of Whit Monday Walks, although declining in many district, was still strong in Pudsey well into the 1920s, in fact the long, snake-like Sunday School processions, curling their way round the town seemed longer than ever. In 1927 the mayor, Simeon Myers, 'a great Sunday School man', planned a new development on the lines of the famous Halifax 'Big Sings'. The venue was Pudsey's cenotaph, the site of the ancient All Saint's chapel-of-ease, then considered the town's most hallowed place. Here all the processions gathered, as well as hundreds of spectators who had flocked into the town, for the 'Big Sing', the climax of which was the Pudsey anthem 'There was a Time when Children Sang'. A glance at the clothes worn by the grown-ups shows that the weather was less clement than hoped for. Yet the rain just held off and according to the local paper, most children 'scorned the protective covering of coats' to reveal 'a riot of colour and all the glory of proudly displayed new dresses and suits'.

32. Pudsey's Manor House from the south in 1900. In 1663 Walter Calverley of Calverley sold the manor of Pudsey to Robert Milner, a large Pudsey landowner whose estate included much of the present town centre. Thereafter the Milner's family home gradually acquired the name of Manor House. The family moved to Kent early in the eighteenth century, although it continued as Lord of the Manor of Pudsey for another hundred and fifty years. The Manor House was let, becoming known as 'The Old Hall'. By the late nineteenth century it had fallen into decay and in 1910 was demolished making way for Trinity Church's new Upper School (plate 26). The house has many seventeenth-century features, elaborate finials at the apex of the gables, drip stones over the windows (to divert the water before gutters and drain pipes were used) and stone mulliened windows. The deep transomed window in the middle bay indicates a house of importance.

33. This photograph of Pudsey's old parsonage must have been taken very shortly before its demolition in 1894. It stood just to the south-east of the ancient All Saint's chapel-of-ease, at the top of the present South Parade. It was described as 'newly built' in 1632, forming the west wing of an existing house. It was built by Elkanah Wales, a famous puritan preacher. Before he died he gave this house, with about twenty acres reaching down towards the present Littlemoor Road, to trustees to augment the income of future Anglican ministers. This land was known as 'glebe land', a name reflected today in Glebe Street. A new parsonage was built in 1832 (plate 34), after which this old parsonage was divided into cottages. The man in the far doorway is John Ross who in 1881 used part of the premises as a lodging house. When the old parsonage was demolished a beautiful decorative plaster ceiling with the date 1647 was also destroyed although the porch and some of the mullioned windows were incorporated into a mens shelter in the park. This shelter was later pulled down to make way for the present aviary.

The Vicarage Pudsey

34. This was Pudsey's second parsonage. By the early nineteenth century the old parsonage seen in plate 33 was considered old-fashioned and damp so in 1831 a new one was built to the north of the newly built St. Lawrence Church. The new parsonage was probably the first house in the district to be planned by an architect. The architect, John Child, designed it specifically as a parsonage, with gothic type windows and two small crosses on the lintel over the front door. John Child was later to become famous as the architect of Leeds' first Roman Catholic Cathedral. The extension at the far end of the parsonage was made in 1870 to accommodate the Rev. Graham's large household, his wife, two servants and seven children. The couple in the foreground are the Rev. French, vicar of Pudsey from 1905 to 1927, and his sister, 'Miss French'. By now you will probably have recognised the house as the original part of the present Airedale Residential Home.

35. This photograph was taken for the benefit of Miss Lilian Dale Copeland, the daughter of the vicar of Pudsey, when she left Pudsey in 1905. Mr. Copeland had two daughters, known to certain parishioners as 'Pussy' and 'Mousie'. Miss Lilian (Pussy), is pictured here, in the hat, with her Young Ladies Class from Radcliffe Lane Sunday School. They are posing at the side of the vicarage (see plate 34), with the two end houses of Park Terrace in the background. Every fortnight Miss Lilian invited her class to the vicarage. Alternate weeks the choirboys came when, after the lesson, they 'had to run of the vicarage, except for the vicar's study'. One thing the choir boys and 'young ladies' remembered throughout their lives was the cage of rabbits next to the stove in the vicarage kitchen.

36. Many Pudsey people do not know of Nesbit Hall, hidden away in trees to the west of Bankhouse, facing south over Fulneck valley. The house has changed little since this photograph was taken just over a hundred years ago, but the field in front is now a bumpy labyrinth of brambles and silver birch. In the late nineteenth century the house was owned by John Cliff of Leeds Fire Clay Company. For about thirty-five years the Company extensively mined the Ing Close in front of the house. Over the years the old tunnels collapsed leaving todays undulating wilderness. The house was originally called Bank House. It was rebuilt, probably in the 1740s, and in 1760 was bought by a London merchant, Claud Nisbet. Although Nisbet died within two years the house remained in the family for about sixty years, much of the time being let to the Moravians of Fulneck. Gradually it acquired the name Nisbet Hall. This soon lapsed into the more pronouncable Nesbit Hall. Claud Nisbet's eldest son, 'Claudie', died mysteriously, his body never having been found. Blood-curling tales are told of it being entombed in the 'lower cellars' of Nesbit Hall.

37. Ninety years ago when this photograph was taken Grove House was occupied by Alfred Lund, worsted spinner of Crawshaw Mills. If you block off the near wing and discount the bay windows you see the original eighteenth century house, neat and symmetrical in design. The house was for many years known as the New Hall, distinguishing it from the old manor house. It was probably built by Joseph Dobson, an attorney and important landowner whose estate stretched northwards to include the present Queens Park. When the house was for sale in 1823 it was suggested that it would make an admirable boarding school! In 1878 it was bought by Pudsey's prosperous boot and shoe manufacturer, William Dibb Scales. He added the Victorian wing and altered the ground floor windows to match. He was remembered as a kind and generous man. Every Whitsuntide all the nonconformist processions queued up to sing for 'Old Scales' at Grove House.

Greenside Tram Terminus.

S. Ormerod
Newsagent Pudsey

38. This three storeyed, or garret, house, seen on the left of plate 10, stood on the corner of Chapeltown and Chapeltown Top. It was demolished in 1931 although Bentleys hairdressers shop on the left remains as a private house. The house was probably built as an inn in the late eighteenth century. It is similar to the old Black Bull and the Fulneck Inn, both now demolished and both built about this time. Its proud corner stones and the stone jambs to the windows support this date. Here in 1833 William Potts came from Durham to establish a clock and watch making business. He remained in Pudsey thirty years, bringing up his seven children and enlarging his business. In the mid-1860s he moved to Leeds where the business continues today as Leeds' only clock manufacturing firm. Most local public clocks were made by this firm. William Potts was succeeded by another clockmaker, Joseph Parker, a local man who specialised in long case clocks with painted dials. He too was successful, having business connections as far afield as Paris.

39. Here is another garret house, but with no stone jambs to the windows and no corner stones. It was built in 1837 by William Hinings and is a typical cloth manufacturer's house of the period. Look closely at the gable end and you can see the blocked up 'taking-in' door. In 1871 the house was bought by Pudsey's Mechanics Institute and for nine years housed the Institute's many activities. When in 1880 the Institute moved to large new premises seen on the left of the picture, the present Town Hall, this spacious house was let to the Central Liberal Club. Then in 1893 it too moved to new premises, the present Liberal Club at the top of Lowtown. This picture was taken just before the house was demolished in 1900 making way for an extension to the Mechanics Institute. The two girls in 'boaters' are probably pupils at the Miss Squires' school which occupied rooms, later used by the public library, in the basement of the Mechanics Institute.

40. The opening of the Church Homes, Tofts Road, in July 1923. The row of six bungalows was designed by Messrs. Nelson & Birkenshaw of Leeds. The homes had all the latest 'mod. cons.', a model combination open fire and cooking stove in the living room, hot and cold water in the bedroom and an indoor WC. The cost, £3,000, was met by Alfred Lund, JP. of Grove House and Crawshaw Mill. The opening was performed by the first Bishop of Bradford, Dr. Perowne. He is on the left of the platform. Next to him in cloak and top hat, is Pudsey's vicar, the Rev. Owen French. The bishop described the homes as 'a permanent memorial to Mr. Lund's abounding generosity'. It was a well deserved accolade as during the ceremony it was announced that he had also given £3,000 to the Church's Fartown Sunday School. Sadly Alfred Lund was unable to be at the opening because of illhealth.

41. These single storeyed cottages were typical of much of Pudsey's poorer housing. They stood in Dyehouse Lane which led from the west end of the Fulneck Terrace into Fulneck valley. The lane was made by the Moravians as a way to their dyehouse by the beck. The 1861 census lists those living in these two tiny dwellings. In the far one lived Robert Glover, a mill watchman, with his wife and six children. No one checked on over-crowding in those days! In the other was Abraham Rhodes, a coalminer from Bowling, who probably worked at one of the pits near Tong. He and his wife had just four children, but they also had a young niece and nephew living with them. This cottage was pulled down shortly after the photograph was taken early this century but the other cottage, still known as 'Glover's House', remained until the 1930s.

42. This photograph of Fulneck valley in flood was taken about a hundred yards upstream from the bottom of Dyehouse Lane, at the place where Abe Lane from Bankhouse crosses the beck to continue up to Tong as Keeper Lane. In 1892 a great storm flooded both the Fulneck and Farnley valleys, washing away bridges and even putting out the fires in the engines houses at Gibraltar and Union Bridge Mills. Notice the bridge crossing the bottom of Keeper Lane. This carried a tramway from Bowling Iron Works, serving a number of pits to the north of Tong. It terminated at an engine house about half a mile to the left of the picture, on Tong Road. This final stretch, part of which can be seen crossing the field, was called the Alexandra Incline. The Company went into liquidation in 1921. The bridge itself has long since gone although the buttresses are still plain to see.

43. About a quarter of a mile upstream from Tong Bridge (plate 42), is another old packhorse way, Scholebrook Lane. Some people still use the old name 'Jack Ass'. Pudsey is particularly rich in these old ways, many of which retain the old causey stones. Jack Ass led from Bankhouse across the valley to Adwalton and beyond. Adwalton was Pudsey's main local fair so this old lane would have witnessed generations of stubborn cattle being driven, and uneasy horses being led to their new homes in Pudsey. The lane was also heavily used by miners tramping to and from Charlie pit which is just over the hill in the picture. Many miners lived in Fartown and were remembered as a rough and hard-drinking lot. There would also be the occasional donkey, or 'Jack Ass', with a pair of panniers hung across its back filled with coal. These beasts were usually driven by young boys who hawked the coal round the Pudsey streets. The stone posts set each side of the bridge were to stop the passage of wheeled traffic.

44. The way up to Stanningley Station from the bottom of Richardshaw Lane in about 1900. The shop on the corner is now Gearys antique shop. Until a branch line was made to Pudsey in 1878 this station was often known as 'Pudsey Station'. It was opened in 1854 with much celebration and cheering. A vast crowd gathered on the platform as the first train from Leeds, with the chairman, directors and shareholders of the Great Northern Railway Company aboard, steamed into the station. Until then the nearest station had been at Calverley Bridge. Within a week of the opening, however, there were complaints. The trains were late, the ticket collectors 'tardy' and the fares too high. A 3rd class ticket to Leeds cost 5d, but coming back it cost 6d! Notice the cabs waiting for hire at the cab stand. These same cabs were periodically used to take patients to Calverley Fever Hospital, then immediately returned to the station for the next fare! The station closed when New Pudsey station opened in 1967.

45. The Great Northern line from Pudsey Greenside Station to Bradford had only been open for six years when this photograph was taken in 1899. The train which has just emerged from the quarter mile long Greenside tunnel, is going under the bridge carrying the track to the Smalewell quarries and is about to run onto the massive embankment, said to be the highest in England, which carried the line across the valley to join the main Leeds-Bradford line at Laisterdyke. The gravelled area in the foreground is where a private track from the quarry connected with the main line to Bradford. The track ran behind the photographer. By 1898 this was a very busy line with sixty trains each day and Lowtown station having fourteen employees and Greenside station twenty-five. But later the line could not compete with motor transport, so it was closed in 1962. Pudsey's Local Board of Health had hoped that when the tunnel and embankment were being constructed some of the tippings could be used to up-grade the old lane across the valley linking Pudsey with Tyersal, but nothing came of the idea.

46. Here is the first tram to Pudsey, in June 1908, just beginning the climb up Richardshaw Lane. The railway viaduct can be seen in the background. The line continued up Church Lane to the terminus by the Commercial Hotel. It was a modest scheme compared to the original plan which was to have covered four and a half miles of Pudsey roads with tram lines. In 1905 a Provisional Order had been granted for the line to continue from Chapeltown as far as Galloway Lane, and for a branch from Druggists Corner (plate 1), to pass along Littlemoor and up Fartown to rejoin the main line at the Commercial. A line to the bottom of Lowtown was also planned. Fortunately a scheme in 1934 to develop the Tong side of Fulneck valley for building which was to have included a road, complete with tramway, running alongside the beck, also failed. Pudsey's tram era lasted just over thirty years, the last tram to Pudsey being in 1939.

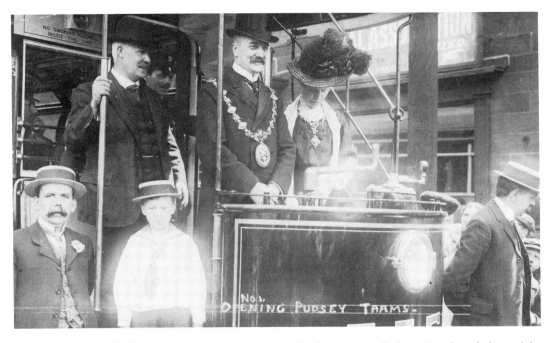

47. This is a better picture of Joseph Huggan, Pudsey's mayor, aboard the first tram to Pudsey. A series of about eight photographs was made of this important occasion. This is No. 1. Joseph Huggan came from an old Lowtown family of handloom weavers. His was one of the few local families to successfully make the transition to powerloom weaving and large scale manufacturing. Joseph Huggan became the senior partner at Swinnow Grange Mills. He lived at Ravensmount, off Littlemoor Road, now the site of a small private housing estate. He was remembered as debonair, well-groomed and always smiling, as in the picture. His young son, Thomas, wearing a boater, was to be killed in the First World War aged just 19 years. The photograph gives a good view of the mayoral chain. It was presented to the Corporation in 1900 by Pudsey's first mayoress, Mrs. James Stillings, in memory of her father, W.D. Scales, whose portrait is incorporated into the chain, just above the pendant. The pendant bears the town's coat of arms. The mayoress' chain was given in 1902 by Pudsey's second mayoress, Mrs. Matthew Walker.

48. Whereas excursion trains were used for outings to the coast wagonettes were a cheap and companiable way of visiting places nearer home. Roundhay Park, Shipley Glen, Knaresborough, Illkley Moor and even Bolton Abbey were all popular destinations. It would be a bumpy ride with solid tyres on the rough, untarmacadamed roads. If it rained a cover was drawn over the passengers and the wagonette would roll along like something out of the wild west. This party are proudly posing in their best outfits outside the Regent Hotel in Fartown in about 1900. The outing is unlikely to have been from the Regent as no respectable woman then went into a public house. In fact it is thought to be from the Fulneck Moravian Church. No details of this outing have been found but in July 1904 for a similar jaunt from Pudsey's Royal Hotel the twenty passengers paid 3s each for a trip to Haworth. The load was pulled by just three horses.

49. Wagonettes, gradually began to be replaced by motor char-à-bancs, like this one. The photograph was taken about eighty years ago, outside the Victoria Hotel at the bottom of Lowtown. The landlord, Frederick William Hepworth, is standing just under the 'Y' of 'Tetley's', wearing a flat cap and moustache. Much later he recalled that this was Samuel Ledgard's first char-à-banc and that the Victoria's first outing in it was to Scarborough. Perhaps this was the occasion of the photograph. The char-à-banc still had solid tyres so the trippers are likely to have looked rather less dapper on their return. Frederick William's wife and little daughter, and the maid, are looking out of the window. Samuel Ledgard developed an extensive business, operating from Armley. One service ran between Leeds and Bradford, through Pudsey. Ledgard buses had a reputation as bone-shakers, but also for always turning up, come snow, ice or fog, when less hardy companies called their buses in. The firm is commemorated in 'Ledgards Way' in Armley.

50. Many people will remember this accident in 1930 when a 'Sammy Leggards' bus ran, backwards, down the bottom of Lowtown right into the living room of the end cottage of Town End Terrace. The Victoria Hotel is in the background. Luckily no one was injured and the house was soon rebuilt but at the time it was an occasion to bring out the Brownie cameras. Town End Terrace, another short row of cottages, and the main road formed a triangle at the bottom of Lowtown with a patch of waste ground in the middle. The cottages, most originally the homes of handloom weavers, were built about 170 years ago on part of the old Crimbles Green, shortly after its enclosure. They are typical of scores of similar sturdy stone cottages which sprang up, 'like seeds scattered unawares' in clusters all over Pudsey. Many, including Town End Terrace, were demolished in the name of slum clearance. Those which survived are becoming increasing up-market, and desirable as 'old weavers cottages'.

51. Just across the road from Town End Terrace was Jim Walker's shop. He began the business in 1898 and this photograph would be taken soon afterwards. A close look at the window shows that as well as being a grocer and greengrocer he also sold pottery, and by 1906 there was a drapery department too. At that time there were no less than twenty-five drapers and sixty-five grocers in Pudsey! Almost every street had its own corner shop. Rabbit skins hanging over the door are waiting to be sold to the visiting skin merchant. Nothing was wasted! Rabbit was then the poor man's chicken but at Christmas Jim Walker sold turkeys at 1s (5p) a pound. In 1902 he took over Lowtown Post Office next door where in January 1909 he distributed the first old age pension, just 5s (25p) a week. Next to Jim Walker is his daughter, Maud, who was born in 1888. The dog was called Jack.

52. No. 5 Lowtown, pictured here, later became Elsters and is now the Help the Aged shop. The career of the founder of Scales & Sons Ltd. is a real rags to riches story. William Dibb Scales was born into a poor family in Armley. He served his apprenticeship as a shoemaker then came to manage his master's two shops in Pudsey, one in Chapeltown and this one in Lowtown. He soon went into partnership with Robert Salter, bought the shops and went on to develop an extensive boot and shoe manufacturing and retailing business with fifty-nine shops throughout the north of England. It was a rule to appoint only Pudsey men as shop managers. W.D. Scales subsequently lived at Grove House and was affectionately remembered as a 'stiff, friendly little man', a great benefactor to Pudsey. On his retirement the firm split, into Salter & Salter and Scales & Sons. Actually he had no sons but five daughters so it was the sons-in-law who continued the business. The firm split again in 1910 with James Stillings taking the trade name 'Stirlings' and Jonathan Webster keeping the family name.

53. This photograph of the Greenside branch of the 'Coop' was taken in the early 1920s. The manager stands proudly in the middle in his distinctive khaki coloured coat. Sometimes he also wore a bowler hat. Inside, the shop was oblong, one side being for 'provisions' (butter, lard, bacon, yeast etc.) with the butter in cwt. barrels and 56 lb. blocks of lard on porcelain dishes on the back counter. The opposite side was the 'dry' side for tea, sugar etc. In a corner, concealed by a display of goods the manager did his accounts. Two tons of flour were delivered each week, the sacks being hauled by crane into the store room above the shop. The flour was then tipped into bins which stretched from floor to ceiling. Those were the days when all self-respecting wives baked their own bread. The shop floor was swept twice a week after which it was covered with sawdust. Then the staff put on clean white smocks, and aprons reaching to the ankles with a frill at the bottom, as in the picture.

BICENTENARY OF MORAVIAN MISSIONS
PAGEANT AT FULNECK. ENGLAND. 1932

PHOTO OVERLAND AIRVIEWS
BRADFORD

54. The next eight photographs are of Fulneck, a unique part of Pudsey. The district was settled by the Moravian brethren, a pre-Reformation protestant church, in the 1740s. Immediately they embarked on an extensive building programme so that most of Fulneck dates from the mid-eighteenth century. This photograph shows the settlement in 1932, revealing how physically detached it was from the rest of the town. The 1748 chapel is in the middle of the long, south-facing Terrace. Standing equi-distant on each side are the twin, pedimented Brethrens and Sisters houses of 1752. These are now incorporated into the Boys and Girls Schools. The last gap in the Terrace was filled in 1923 when a two storeyed extension to the Girls School was built immediately opposite Charles Sebastian Nelson's house, spoiling his view across Fulneck valley (plate 58). Today the Terrace's historical and architectural importance is recognised in its being 'listed' Grade 1.

55. The East Terrace, Fulneck. At first glance this scene has altered little in the eighty years or so since the photograph was taken. But look closer and you will see that beyond Fulneck End was still open fields. Then in 1927 the Southroyd housing estate was built. Initially the estate was nationally renowned for houses which could be rented for just 5s a week. The building on the right, now demolished, and the long, low building opposite were probably built in 1783 as part of a planned residential Square for Fulneck. One building was to be a porter's lodge and the other a day school for Pudsey children. Little of the Square materialised and these two buildings soon became cottages. The one on the right had steps leading to the upper storey. About a hundred years ago this was used as a workroom by 'Tailor Gaunt'. Later he and his son, Mazzini, moved across the road. In the tiny cottage beneath lived Dickey Hardaker, renowned as Pudsey St. Lawrence's 'stumper', and also as a fiddler.

56. These are the cottages in the distance, on the left of plate 55. A hundred years ago there were two cottages here. The roof timbers suggest the cottage on the left is the older. It has a vertical kingpost from the middle of the tie beam reaching to the apex of the roof, a feature which disappeared in the mid-eighteenth century. In 1871 George Swales, a tanner at Goodall's tannery, lived here with a young girl who he would have people believe he was trying to reform. After his death the cottage became Mazzini Gaunt's tailor's workshop. Charles Mazzini was always very smart, very erect. He wore a distinctive hat, tall, broad and square shaped. Next door Bob Proctor, a farmer, brought up his three children. On his death the cottages decayed, part being used as Fred Stott's green-grocery store (he had a 'round' rather than a shop), and part a bicycle shed. This is probably when this picture was taken. But since 1970 the cottages have been transformed into Brian Halliday's 'Serendipity', a Mecca for flower arrangers.

57. This is the west end of Fulneck in 1902 with the shop and warehouse in the foreground. The shop moved to these premises in 1771 when Jeremiah Haley was appointed, by Lot, as shopkeeper. The shop sold everything you could possibly want, garters, herrings, comfits, glass buttons, spades, stockings, habit gloves, smelling bottles, whalebone, coffin attire, brass handles, muslin and tenter hooks. The shop also supplied the Pudsey workhouse with vast quantities of tobacco, treacle and hops. The original shop sign was still in situ when this picture was taken. The shop now serves primarily as the school tuck shop and as a café and restaurant. Next door is the old warehouse, lately Mollie Hillam's pottery. Since her recent tragic death in a road accident the building awaits another role. Beyond are the upper storeys of some 'family houses'. On the other side these are two storeyed, facing south across the valley and aptly called 'Paradise'.

58. About ninety years ago, when this photograph was taken, the Moravian Whit Walk assembled on the Terrace. After singing at traditional stops at the west end of the village the younger children went to the Boys Sunday School, the present Comenius Centre, for the first sitting down of tea. So when the singers arrived at No. 29 the picture shows that only the older children and adults remained. This was where Mr. Nelson lived. Charles Sebastian Nelson has been encountered many times in this book as a local architect. He was also the 'Peter Pan' of Fulneck. It was said that he played the Fulneck organ for ninety of his ninety-two years! Today this house, now called Nelson House, is part of the Girls School. In the photograph it is just possible to discern two stringed instruments leading the singing. Later the Fulneck Whit Walks were accompanied by a harmonium strapped to a hand cart.

59. Pudsey's 2nd Company of the Boys Brigade, the Fulneck Company, was formed in 1894, just a year after the company attached to Pudsey's Congregational Church. The latter lapsed for a time but the Fulneck Company continued without a break and was proud of its title, the 2nd Leeds Company. This photograph was probably taken about 1907. In the background is the former Fulneck Inn. As Fulneck was the centre for all the Yorkshire Moravian congregations, and also for many years the only Moravian place of burial, an inn was an essential adjunct to 'The Place', as Fulneck was, and still is, called. The three-storeyed building dates from 1761. Until the advent of the temperance movement in the 1830s it was fully licensed, providing wine, punch, rum and brandy, as well as home-brewed ale. But from 1848 no licensed inns were allowed in Moravian settlements. Thereafter it was a temperance hotel, and by 1900 'The Morningside Guest House', it faced east for the morning sun. About forty years ago it became the music department for the Boys' School, but on Christmas Eve 1968 it collapsed into a heap of rubble.

60. Fulneck had its own fire engine at least fifty years before Pudsey. The first engine was acquired in 1779 although this one dates from 1822. Its crew of thirteen included the captain, engineer, deputy engineer, secretary, hydrant attendant and knocker-up. Member's loyalty in attending the four-monthly trials was encouraged by the prospect of 'a good substantial supper' following the winter trial. The last fire attended by the crew was in 1890, a blaze in the 'Ladies School' sitting room. But by the time seven firemen had been mustered and the engine extracted from its shelter under Daniel Hutton's shop, seen in the background of the picture, the fire was out. Thereafter the trials degenerated into comic entertainments when windows were washed. Soon the engine was left to decay, only to be rediscovered, and restored within the last thirty years. It is now in Fulneck Museum, respendent in its original 1822 livery of green and vermilion. Standing on the right of the picture, with moustache, white shirt and tie, is Len Hutton's father.

61. For over two hundred years the Moravians boarding and day schools at Fulneck have been part of the childhood of many Pudsey children. The Girls School came to Pudsey in 1755, the Boys School had come two years before. Initially they were for the children of Moravian ministers, many of whom were abroad as missionaries, but by the end of the eighteenth century they were taking fee-paying children. This delightful photograph of the Girls School is taken in the Parsonage garden, sometime between 1901 and 1904. There were then about forty boarders and ten day girls. The school was housed under, and to the east of the chapel, the main rooms opening onto the long, south-facing Terrace. The dormitory was above the chapel. In 1904 the school moved into the Sisters House and a new building which included a lecture hall. This forms the nucleus of the Girls School today. A future headmistress, Miss Curry, then a young assistant teacher, is sitting on the extreme right of the photograph.

62. This photograph is taken outside the Methodist's Lower Sunday School on Crimbles. The building was used during the week by the Crimbles Board School. The infants occupied Pudsey Church's Lowtown Sunday School. Although Pudsey's School Board was formed in 1876 it was some time before all the Board Schools were purpose built. The children in the photograph are in their Sunday best for the occasion. Normally they would wear pinafores, with plain dresses underneath, for school. Alice Walker, sister to Maud (plate 51), is on the left on the top row. Her half yearly reports show that in the three Rs, composition, geography and sewing she was 'Very Good'. Her conduct was 'Excellent'. But her attendance at school was consistently 'Not Satisfactory'. In fact she was often kept at home to help with the cooking and housework. She was not alone in her poor attendance. About one in three children were absent each day!

The Council School.

S. Ormerod
News Agent, Pudsey.

63. Richardshaw Lane School, opened in 1877, was Pudsey's first purpose-built Board School. There was an Infant School in the middle with a Boys and a Girls School on each side, in all accommodating six hundred children. On the right is the Masters House and School Board offices. Pudsey was very proud of its new school, 'pleasantly situated at the top of a hill with an uninterrupted view extending as far as Rombalds Moor'. It was before the Cemetery Road and 'Building Field' developments. But the first head-mistress had a hard time. She had just two pupil teachers to help teach six 'Standards'. Sometimes on the frequent occasions when the pupil teachers were away ill she had to take the whole school of two hundred herself. At one time a young pupil teacher was left with a class of seventy-five for a week. Fortunately conditions gradually improved. This photograph, probably taken around 1930, shows some of the children on waste ground, now occupied by flats, opposite the school.

64. These well-groomed children are members of Luther Gaunt's violin class at Primrose Hill School. The photograph was probably taken soon after the school was opened in 1899. School violin classes were not uncommon at this time. They were sponsored by a violin manufacturing firm. The children paid 6d a week towards the 25s for the violin, bow and case, as well at 6d for the actual lesson. So it was only the more favoured children who benefited. Luther Gaunt, with his brother Ernest (who taught the piano and organ), had a private music school in Brunswick Terrace. Primrose Hill School was built on the most modern lines. Instead of children being grouped in various corners of one large room, as in earlier Board Schools, there were separate classrooms. 'Pimmys' was chosen as the one Pudsey school to have a Standard 7. This developed into a pupil teacher centre which in 1905 moved to the newly opened Higher Grade School then held in the Mechanies Institute, the present Town Hall. This in turn was the forerunner of Pudsey Secondary (later Grammar) School.

NEW SECONDARY & TECHNICAL SCHOOL PUDSEY OPENED SEPT. 1910

65. Pudsey's Higher Grade School had by 1906 developed into a Secondary School and Pupil Teacher centre. The number of pupils rose steadily, from seventy-five in 1904 to 150 in 1908 so more spacious premises than rooms in the Mechanics Institute became essential. In 1910 therefore Pudsey's Secondary & Technical School was transferred to this fine new building, the present Grangefield School, designed by Jowett, Kendall & Son. It cost £18,000 and accommodated over three hundred pupils. The two girls in the foreground are probably wearing the original school uniform. Mr. Samuel Sawyer, the first headmaster, was to remain until 1934 at what became known as Pudsey Grammar School. He was remembered as 'a typical schoolmaster, but with a twinkle in his eye to inspire confidence and respect rather than fear'.

66. This is Pudsey's fire brigade, taking part in the mile long procession to celebrate Pudsey's Charter of Incorporation on 13th November 1899. The Charter arrived unexpectedly early so there was less than a week to organise the celebrations, the procession, teas for all the children (mugs of tea and bags of buns, sweetbread and fruit), and a massive fire work display when it was estimated 30,000 people packed into the Recreation Ground. Pudsey fire brigade was a regular at civic occasions. There were two engines, the horse-drawn steam engine probably dating from 1868, pictured here, and the old manual engine which was like the Fulneck engine (plate 60). It was powered by pumping on the handles and used when there were problems with the steam engine, such as catching the horses. The horses grazed in Cabby Wood's field on Cemetery Road. The houses in the background, on the corner of Greenside and Station Street, were the only houses in Pudsey to be bombed during the Second World War.

67. Pudsey's Charter was little more than a year old when Edward VII was proclaimed King in February 1901. Civic pride and fervour were still intense so the Proclamation was an excuse for another high civic occasion. A special platform was erected in the Recreation Ground for the VIPs, the mayor, aldermen, councillors, members of the School Board, the Poor Law guardians, representatives from the Mechanics Institute, ministers of religion and the mace bearer. The Pudsey Borough Band and the Richardshaw Lane Band, augmented by military buglars, marched through the town announcing the imminent Proclamation. The result was this massive crowd, estimated at about six thousand. And this despite a cold, bleak, snowy February day. You can see Hutton Terrace in the background and Crawshaw Mill chimney is on the extreme left.

Pudsey Bonfire June 22 191 HWA

68. Pudsey celebrated the Coronation of George V in June 1911 with this massive bonfire on Greentop. It was thirty feet high and sixty feet in circumference, its erection having been supervised by a local architect, William Shackleton. A similar picture in the local paper shows a Union Jack flying from the top, reached by a ladder with workmen precariously poised half way up. The bonfire was the climax of a day of celebration. In the morning the town council and other 'public bodies' had processed from the new Secondary School to the parish church for a service. The afternoon saw a grand procession of local organisations culminating in sports, entertainments and fireworks provided by the mayor, Alderman Walter Forrest of Meadowhurst. Finally at 10pm the flag was lowered from the bonfire and the stack lit by Pudsey's Highway Surveyor. Soon there was a magnificent blaze, said to have been seen as far away as Lancashire and York, although this would have been hard to prove as the night was ablaze with bonfires on hilltops in all directions.

69. One of Pudsey's proud possessions was its steam roller. The original steam roller dated from about 1906. It was nicknamed The Potato Squasher. But as horses began to give way to heavy motor traffic tarmacadamed roads were introduced and a heavier steam roller was needed. Moreover by 1921 there were major road improvements in the pipeline, especially in Chapeltown around the new cenotaph and a new road was needed to reach Pudsey's first council housing estate at Heath Grove in Uppermoor. At first the Council, reluctant to saddle the ratepayers with a bill for £1,500, contemplated hiring a roller. But town pride prevailed and in the autumn of 1921 Pudsey acquired this handsome new roller, fully equipped for tar spraying and made by Fowlers of Leeds. The photograph is taken in front of the Fire Station, the present Pudsey House. On the extreme right is Alderman John Keighley, next to him is Harry Sharp, fifth from the right is Luther Sunderland, next in the trilby is Dr. Byrd and next to him is George Womersley.

70. Pudsey's first carnival was in July 1898. Never before had the town been so profusely decorated with bunting, streamers and flags, with banners stretched across the street proclaiming 'Success to our Carnival' and 'May Pudsey Prosper'. The mammoth procession had started at the Recreation Ground, proceeded down Lowtown, along Swinnow, up Lowtown and Church Lane to Chapeltown and Greenside. The photographer, Lewis Schofield, lived at the Greenside end of Smalewell Road from where this picture (and plate 66) was taken. The procession then went down Fartown, along Littlemoor Road, up Radcliffe Lane and Chapeltown (again) to finish up at the Marsh Ground. The picture shows the carnival president, James Stillings, with his wife (W.D. Scales's daughter), in their coach decorated with 250 yellow paper roses. Two years later he was to become Pudsey's first mayor.

71. The carnival lapsed after 1900. In 1907 therefore Pudsey's Lifeboat Committee determined to make Lifeboat Saturday a worthy substitute. It certainly achieved the nature of a carnival with the route of the procession gay with streamers and flags. There were the stalwarts of the old carnivals, Pudsey's Fire Brigade, local brass bands, the carriages of local worthies, the British Women's Temperance Assocation, local Friendly Societies and the newly formed St. John's Ambulance Brigade. The pièce de résistance, however, was the Worthing lifeboat, manned by the Scarborough lifeboat crew and drawn by seven splendidly harnessed horses from Barraclough's foundry. After a comprehensive perambulation of the town the lifeboat was launched, nine feet, into Leigh Mills dam, drenching the watchings VIPs. This unusual spectacle was witnessed by crowds gathered on Owlcotes and along Cemetery Road. The event was never repeated. This is yet another photograph taken from the end of Smalewell Road, where the photographer, Lewis Schofield, lived.

72. Pudsey's carnival was revived in 1923 and this photograph would be taken shortly afterwards. It shows a modest float, presumably bound for the carnival, on Fulneck Street, then still cobbled. 'An Eskimo Village' was an appropriate subject for the Moravians as for many years they had had widespread mission stations amongst the eskimos of Labrador. On the left is the young Len Hutton who was born and brought up in Fulneck.

73. A major omission so far in this collection of photographs of 'Old Pudsey' is of people's working lives. The last four pictures attempt to rectify this. Here is the culmination of the hay harvest at Sam Moss's farm at Wood Nook. Much of his land now lies under the Stanningley by-pass. It was a typical local farm with cows, wheat, hay, turnips and, for a time, rhubarb. Every year at haytime and harvest the Irish came. A regular at Wood Nook was Big Michael who was happy to doss down at night in a recently vacated pig sty. The picture shows Sam Moss with his helpers, along with various children there for the fun and women in hats, apparently there primarily to have their photographs taken. Or they may have just brought the 'Drinkings' up to the field. A glance at a map of Pudsey in the 1920s shows that much of Pudsey was still open fields. Agriculture was still an important industry.

74. Pudsey's Borough Cabinet Works were built in Occupation Lane in 1897. William Davy had begun the business in 1880 in Greenside. As the business grew he moved into an old handloom weaving 'factory' at Waterloo Mills. But a disastrous fire in 1897 in which he lost machinery and stock worth £5,000 forced him to find new premises. Fortunately he was fully insured. Nevertheless the decision to build the vast workplace seen above was a brave venture. William Davy introduced electrical power when it was still in its infancy so that the premises were said to 'surpass any place of its kind for many miles around'. The firm specialised in medium class furniture, mostly sideboards and bedroom suites. William Davy died in 1905 when just fifty-two years old. The business then passed to his son-in-law, J.W. Boyd. Inevitably the firm suffered in the slump of the 1920s. This was exacerbated by Mr. Boyd's generosity in taking on the unemployed so that in 1929 the business was forced into voluntary liquidation. Since then the premises have been occupied by E. Jones & Sons, cornmerchants, but have recently been demolished.

75. The last two photographs illustrate Pudsey's staple industry, wool textiles. This picture is of New Shed Mills in New Street, taken from the present Glebe Mount. Many people will remember the engine house on New Street where, as the door was usually open, you could see the massive boiler and gleaming pipes, the power house of this large complex of firms. New Shed Mills was built in 1871 by the Pudsey Worsted Mill Co., with 1,700 shares at the low price of £2 each enabling working men to become shareholders. It was a 'room and power' mill, various firms renting accommodation, and power from the central engine. The mill was confined to weaving, mostly of worsteds. In 1910, probably about when this picture was taken, there were eight firms with over six hundred looms in the complex, twice as many looms as in any other Pudsey mill. L.J. Walker & Co. had forty-eight looms. (You can just see the firm's name on the side of the cart.) The firm had a world-wide reputation for its worsted coatings.

76. This float belongs to Priestley Mill, a large woollen mill dating back to 1834 which, until a few years ago, stood on the site of the present Priestley housing estate at Lane End. With the aid of a magnifying glass you can see a portrait of Queen Alexandra on the top of the display suggesting that the float was about to take part in the procession to celebrate the Coronation of Edward VII in 1902. Samuel Cordingley, probably the elderly man in the photograph, bought Priestley Mill in 1888 and built Priestley House, seen here, nearby. The son of a Calverley master tailor he began his own business as a handloom weaver, eventually moving to Airedale Mill at Rodley. This final picture well illustrates three rich characteristics of 'Old Pudsey', its native textile industry, its wealth of solidly built stone houses and its civic pride which was vigorously expressed in its predisposition for large, elaborate displays, carnivals and processions.